Caring for Our Li

Our classroom has a new pet.
Our new pet is a lizard.

We can take care of our lizard.
What does he need?

People need homes.
Our lizard needs a home to keep him safe.

We can give him a home!

People need fresh air to breathe.
Our lizard needs fresh air too.

We can give him some fresh air.

We need light so we can see.
Our lizard needs light too.

We can give him some light.

What else does our lizard need?
He needs heaters to keep him warm.

We can give him some heaters.

People need good food to eat.
Our lizard needs good food too.

We can give him some good food.

We need clean water to drink.
Our lizard needs clean water too.

We can give him some clean water.
Does our lizard have everything he needs?

No! Our lizard needs a name.
His name is Lenny.